Practical
Smoothies & Juices

p^3

This is a P³ Book
First published in 2003

P³
Queen Street House
4 Queen Street
Bath BA1 1HE, UK

ISBN: 1-40540-939-8

Printed in China

NOTE

Cup measurements in this book are for American cups.
This book also uses imperial and metric measurements. Follow the same units
of measurement throughout; do not mix imperial and metric.
All spoon measurements are level: teaspoons are assumed to be 5 ml, and
tablespoons are assumed to be 15 ml. Unless otherwise stated,
milk is assumed to be whole milk, eggs and individual vegetables such as potatoes
are medium, and pepper is freshly ground black pepper.

Optional ingredients, variations, or serving suggestions have not been
included in the calculations. The times given for each recipe are an approximate
guide only because the preparation times may differ according to the techniques used by
different people and the cooking times may vary as a result of the type of oven used.

Recipes using raw or very lightly cooked eggs should be
avoided by infants, the elderly, pregnant women, convalescents,
and anyone suffering from an illness.

Contents

Introduction

It is no surprise that smoothies and mixed juices have become so fashionable in these health-conscious days. Commercial soft drinks and even some fruit juices often contain ingredients that many of us would rather avoid—artificial colors and flavorings, high levels of sugar or chemical sweeteners, and preservatives. In addition, many commercially produced drinks taste so artificial, bland, or unexciting that they simply do not appeal to today's discerning palate.

Making drinks from fruit and vegetables at home ensures that we know precisely what they contain. It also means that we can mix them to taste truly delicious, and we can guarantee that the raw ingredients are organic, if that is what we want.

Nutritionists recommend that we should eat at least five portions of fruit and vegetables a day. Modern life is so busy, however, that few of us have the time or inclination to plan, buy, prepare, and cook balanced meals every day of the week. The good news is that, in the few minutes it takes to juice a handful of carrots and tomatoes, or to whizz some berries and yogurt in the food processor, we can produce the equivalent of one of those portions. Better still, the ingredients are usually raw and the drink will be consumed immediately, so there is less possibility of losing nutrients during cooking or through excessive exposure to air. This makes the drink healthier.

You can make smoothies and juices from most fruit and vegetables. The golden rule is never to combine the two, with the exception of apples, carrots, and tomatoes. The recipes in this book will give you an excellent starting point, and should provide you with lots of ideas for inventing your own drinks. Generally, once people have begun the habit of making their own drinks in this way, they become great enthusiasts and never feel the need to return to commercial brands.

Smoothies and juices are very enjoyable thirst quenchers, but there is much more to them than this. Many provide a powerful boost that can give a kick-start at breakfast time or revive flagging energy in the afternoon, with a healthy nutritional balance that will not be found in a packet of cookies or a chocolate bar.

Apples, for example, are a powerhouse of slow-releasing carbohydrate, the kind that keeps you going for several hours. Citrus fruits, berries, and, above all, kiwifruit are packed with vitamin C. Strawberries and raspberries contain iron, and carrots are a valuable source of beta-carotene. In addition, if you use a juicer (see opposite), fiber is incorporated into the drink and not discarded.

The selection of delicious drinks in this book includes not only smoothies and mixed juices, but also coolers and other long drinks, pick-me-ups and energy boosters, tea- and coffee-based mixes, and some irresistible milkshakes for a special treat. You will also find opposite some useful information about equipment, such as how to choose the right juicer to suit your budget, and ways of preparing ingredients to set you on the right path to complete success in making your own healthy and tasty fruit and vegetable concoctions.

Making smoothies and juices is great fun, as well as being very healthy. All you need are the right equipment and ingredients, some recipes, and your imagination.

Equipment

You do not have to spend a lot of money on equipment, but for the best and freshest results, you will need a food processor and a juicer.

A basic kitchen food processor with a standard metal blade mixes smoothies to perfection in a few moments, and the recipes in this book assume that one will be used. You might also be able to use a blender, depending on the sturdiness of the model. However, unless your food processor has a juicer attachment, you cannot use it for making juice, because it will simply turn the ingredients into a puree. A juicer, on the other hand, separates the pulp from the juice. There are three types of juicer, and these vary considerably in price. Centrifugal juicers are at the lower end of the price range. Coarsely chopped ingredients are fed into this juicer, which grates them into tiny pieces and spins them at high speed. The liquid is extracted by centrifugal force, leaving the fruit or vegetable pulp behind. Fruit and vegetables are exposed to the air during this process, so juices made by this method are thought to have the lowest nutritional content.

Hydraulic juicers are at the top end of the price range. Extreme pressure forces the juice out of the ingredients, through a strainer, and into a pitcher, leaving the pulp behind. Juices pressed by this method are very high in nutrients.

The third type, triturating juicers, are in the middle of the range in terms of price and nutritional value. In these, a rotating cutter tears up the ingredients and presses them through a strainer.

Besides cost, other aspects to consider before buying a juicer are size—triturating juicers tend to be larger than the others—the speed at which they work, and how easy they are to clean. But whichever type of juicer you choose, you can still be sure that the drink you are creating will be full of nutrients as well as flavor.

Any other equipment you are likely to need, from a cutting board to an ice-cube tray, you will almost certainly already have in your pantry.

When you use a food processor, everything that goes into the bowl will be incorporated into the drink, so fruit and vegetables must be washed, peeled, and prepared in the same way as for any other type of recipe. Pits and seeds must all be removed. Large, firm fruit and vegetables, such as apples and carrots, should be coarsely chopped before being processed.

Techniques

If you are going to add ice cubes to the food processor, crush them first to avoid damaging the blade. You can do this by wrapping them in a clean dish towel and hammering them with a meat mallet or rolling pin. The technique with juicers, whatever type you are using, is different because the juice and solid residue are kept separate. Most vegetables and fruits, with the exception of bananas, kiwifruit, and citrus fruits, do not need to be peeled. However, they should still be thoroughly washed.

Some juicers can cope with quite tough skins, even melon skins. Many of the nutrients in fruits lie just below the surface of the skin, so this is a particularly valuable asset, but it does mean that you must be sure to use specimens with undamaged skins.

As a rough guide to making your own fresh juices, remember that 1 lb 2 oz/500 g of raw carrots or apples will produce scant 1 cup of juice, while 1 lb 2 oz/500 g of tomatoes or blackberries will produce scant 1½ cups.

You can leave vegetable tops, such as beet leaves, attached, but do trim off the roots. Coarse outer leaves that would normally be removed for other culinary purposes do not need trimming. Pits, such as those in cherries, peaches, and mangoes, should be removed, but you can leave smaller seeds in grapes, apples, and pears. The process of making the juice is then very simple.

Melon Medley

This summer smoothie, with three different kinds of melon, is deliciously refreshing on a hot day.

SERVES 2

I N G R E D I E N T S

1 cup plain yogurt

¾ cup honeydew melon, coarsely chopped

¾ cup cantaloupe melon, coarsely chopped

¾ cup watermelon, coarsely chopped

6 ice cubes

wedges of melon, to decorate

1 Pour the yogurt into a food processor. Add the honeydew melon pieces and process until smooth.

2 Add the cantaloupe and watermelon pieces along with the ice cubes and process until smooth. Pour the mixture into glasses and decorate with wedges of melon. Serve at once.

Fruit Cooler

Power up with breakfast in a glass, packed with protein, vitamins, and slow-release carbohydrate—and a sensational flavor, too.

SERVES 2

INGREDIENTS

1 cup orange juice

½ cup plain yogurt

2 eggs

2 bananas, sliced and frozen

slices of fresh banana, to decorate

1 Pour the orange juice and yogurt into a food processor and process gently until combined.

2 Add the eggs and frozen banana slices and process until smooth. Pour the mixture into glasses and decorate the rims with slices of fresh banana. Add straws and serve.

Pacific Smoothie

Luscious figs combine superbly with the nuts, orange juice, and maple syrup in this unusual and delicate drink.

SERVES 2

I N G R E D I E N T S

1½ cups hazelnut yogurt

2 tbsp freshly squeezed orange juice

4 tbsp maple syrup

8 large fresh figs, chopped

6 ice cubes

toasted chopped hazelnuts, to decorate

1 Pour the yogurt, orange juice, and maple syrup into a food processor and process gently until combined.

2 Add the figs and ice cubes and process until smooth. Pour the mixture into glasses and scatter over some toasted chopped hazelnuts to decorate. Serve at once.

Red Bell Pepper Reactor

Boost your energy levels and fire up your system with this truly dynamic fruit-and-vegetable medley.

I N G R E D I E N T S

1 cup carrot juice

1 cup tomato juice

2 large red bell peppers, seeded and coarsely chopped

1 tbsp lemon juice

pepper

1 Pour the carrot juice and tomato juice into a food processor and process gently until combined.

2 Add the bell peppers and lemon juice. Season with plenty of freshly ground black pepper and process until smooth. Pour the mixture into tall glasses, add straws, and serve.

Ginger Crush

The sweet, mild flavors of carrot and tomato
are literally gingered up in this enlivening drink.

SERVES 2

I N G R E D I E N T S

1 cup carrot juice

4 tomatoes, skinned, seeded, and
  coarsely chopped

1 tbsp lemon juice

½ cup coarsely chopped fresh parsley

1 tbsp grated fresh gingerroot

6 ice cubes

½ cup water

chopped fresh parsley, to garnish

1 Put the carrot juice, tomatoes, and
  lemon juice in a food processor and
process gently until combined.

2 Add the parsley to the food processor
  along with the ginger and ice cubes.
Process until well combined, then pour
in the water and process until smooth.

3 Pour the mixture into tall glasses and
  garnish with chopped fresh parsley.
Serve at once.

Nectarine Melt

Mango and nectarine form an inspired combination, made all the more special with the clever addition of lemon sherbet.

INGREDIENTS

1 cup milk

2 cups lemon sherbet

1 ripe mango, pitted and diced

2 ripe nectarines, pitted and diced

1 Pour the milk into a food processor, add half of the lemon sherbet, and process gently until combined. Add the remaining lemon sherbet and then process until smooth.

2 When the mixture is thoroughly blended, gradually add the mango and nectarines and process until smooth. Pour the mixture into glasses, add straws, and serve.

Peppermint Ice

Simultaneously minty and creamy on the tongue, this classic combination still manages to pack a surprise.

SERVES 2

INGREDIENTS

⅔ cup milk

2 tbsp peppermint syrup

2 cups peppermint ice cream

sprigs of fresh mint, to decorate

1 Pour the milk and peppermint syrup into a food processor and process gently until combined.

2 Add the peppermint ice cream and process until smooth. Pour the mixture into tall glasses and decorate with sprigs of fresh mint. Add straws and serve.

Orange & Lime Iced Tea

Sweet and sharp citrus flavors turn a very simple drink into a subtle and sophisticated thirst quencher.

SERVES 2

INGREDIENTS

1¼ cups water

2 tea bags

scant ½ cup orange juice

4 tbsp lime juice

1–2 tbsp brown sugar

8 ice cubes

TO DECORATE

wedge of lime

sugar

slices of fresh orange, lemon, or lime

1 Pour the water into a pan and bring to a boil. Remove from the heat, add the tea bags, and let infuse for 5 minutes. Remove the tea bags and let the tea cool to room temperature (about 30 minutes). Transfer to a pitcher, cover with plastic wrap, and chill in the refrigerator for at least 45 minutes.

2 When the tea has chilled, pour in the orange juice and lime juice. Add sugar to taste.

3 Take two glasses and rub the rims with a wedge of lime, then dip them in sugar to frost. Put the ice cubes into the glasses and pour over the tea. Decorate the rims with slices of fresh orange, lemon, or lime, and serve.

Berry Cream

The inspired combination of sweet banana and tart summer berries could almost be described as intoxicating.

SERVES 2

INGREDIENTS

1½ cups orange juice

1 lb/450 g frozen berries, such as blueberries, raspberries, and blackberries

1 banana, sliced and frozen

slices of fresh strawberry, to decorate

1 Pour the orange juice into a food processor. Add half of the frozen berries and all the banana slices and process until smooth.

2 Add the remaining berries and process until smooth. Pour the mixture into tall glasses and decorate the rims with slices of fresh strawberry. Add straws and serve.

Banana & Blueberry Smoothie

Sweet, sharp, fragrant, rich, and creamy, this is pure magic in a glass that will lift your spirits.

SERVES 2

INGREDIENTS

¾ cup apple juice

½ cup plain yogurt

1 banana, sliced and frozen

1 cup frozen blueberries

whole fresh blueberries, to decorate

1 Pour the apple juice into a food processor. Add the yogurt and process until smooth.

2 Add the frozen banana slices and half of the frozen blueberries and process well, then add the remaining frozen blueberries and process until smooth. Pour the mixture into tall glasses and decorate with whole fresh blueberries. Add straws and serve.

Strawberry Sunrise

Probably one of the first smoothies ever invented,
this impeccable combination remains a firm favorite.

SERVES 2

INGREDIENTS

½ cup plain yogurt

¾ cup strawberry yogurt

¾ cup orange juice

generous ½ cup frozen sliced strawberries

1 banana, sliced and frozen

TO DECORATE

slices of fresh orange

whole fresh strawberries

1 Pour the plain and strawberry yogurts into a food processor and process gently. Add the orange juice and process until the mixture is combined.

2 Add the frozen strawberries and banana slices and process until smooth. Pour the mixture into tall glasses and decorate with slices of fresh orange and whole fresh strawberries. Add straws and serve.

Summer & Citrus Fruit Punch

Serve this vibrant punch whenever you have something to celebrate, or just to make yourself feel good.

SERVES 2

INGREDIENTS

4 tbsp orange juice

1 tbsp lime juice

scant ½ cup sparkling water

2 cups frozen summer fruits (such as blueberries, raspberries, blackberries, and strawberries)

4 ice cubes

whole fresh raspberries, black currants or blueberries, and blackberries, threaded alternately on toothpicks, to decorate

1 Pour the orange juice, lime juice, and sparkling water into a food processor and process gently until combined.

2 Add the frozen summer fruits and ice cubes and process until a slushy consistency has been reached.

3 Pour the mixture into glasses. Decorate with whole fresh raspberries, black currants or blueberries, and blackberries, threaded alternately on toothpicks, and serve immediately.

Strawberry & Peach Smoothie

One luscious glassful of this marvelously fruity mix and you will feel restored, revived, and refreshed.

SERVES 2

INGREDIENTS

¾ cup milk

8 oz/225 g canned peach slices, drained

2 fresh apricots, chopped

12–14 fresh strawberries, hulled and sliced

2 bananas, sliced and frozen

slices of fresh strawberries, to decorate

1 Pour the milk into a food processor. Add the peach slices and process gently until combined. Add the apricots and process gently until combined.

2 Add the strawberries and banana slices and process until smooth. Pour the mixture into glasses and then decorate the rims with slices of fresh strawberries. Serve at once.

Fruit Rapture

Simple, but splendid, this restorative smoothie will get you back on track at any time of day.

INGREDIENTS

scant ½ cup milk

½ cup peach yogurt

scant ½ cup orange juice

8 oz/225 g canned peach slices, drained

6 ice cubes

strips of fresh orange zest, to decorate

1 Pour the milk, yogurt, and orange juice into a food processor and process gently until combined.

2 Add the peach slices and ice cubes and process until smooth. Pour the mixture into glasses and then decorate with strips of fresh orange zest. Add straws and serve.

Spicy Banana Chill

A Caribbean combo to tantalize the taste buds with just a hint of heat in every mouthful of icy sweetness.

SERVES 2

I N G R E D I E N T S

1¼ cups milk

½ tsp mixed spice

¾ cup banana ice cream

2 bananas, sliced and frozen

1 Pour the milk into a food processor and add the mixed spice. Add half of the banana ice cream and process gently until combined, then add the remaining ice cream and process until well blended.

2 When the mixture is well combined, add the frozen banana slices and process until smooth. Pour the mixture into tall glasses, add straws, and then serve at once.

Banana & Coffee Milkshake

This unusual milkshake is a powerhouse drink for those who lead life on the run and tastes delicious, too.

SERVES 2

INGREDIENTS

1¼ cups milk

4 tbsp instant coffee powder

¾ cup vanilla ice cream

2 bananas, sliced and frozen

1 Pour the milk into a food processor, add the coffee powder, and process gently until combined. Add half of the vanilla ice cream and process gently, then add the remaining ice cream and process until well combined.

2 When the mixture is thoroughly blended, add the frozen banana slices and process until smooth. Pour the mixture into glasses and serve.

Rich Chocolate Shake

This is the ultimate milkshake for children and chocoholics of all ages, and is supremely satisfying.

SERVES 2

INGREDIENTS

⅔ cup milk

2 tbsp chocolate syrup

2 cups chocolate ice cream

grated chocolate, to decorate

1 Pour the milk and chocolate syrup into a food processor and process gently until combined.

2 Add the chocolate ice cream and process until smooth. Pour the mixture into tall glasses and decorate by floating the grated chocolate on top. Serve at once.

Maple & Almond Milkshake

Go on. Why not indulge your sweet tooth with this irresistible, rich-tasting, novel milkshake?

SERVES 2

I N G R E D I E N T S

⅔ cup milk

2 tbsp maple syrup

2 cups vanilla ice cream

1 tbsp almond extract

chopped almonds, to decorate

1 Pour the milk and maple syrup into a food processor and process gently until combined.

2 Add the ice cream and almond extract and process until smooth. Pour the mixture into glasses and decorate with the chopped almonds. Add straws and serve.

Kiwi Dream

This drink gives you an excellent intake of vitamin C in a glass, as well as a marvelously refreshing sweet and sharp flavor.

SERVES 2

INGREDIENTS

⅔ cup milk

juice of 2 limes

2 kiwifruit, peeled and chopped

1 tbsp sugar

2 cups vanilla ice cream

TO DECORATE

slices of fresh kiwifruit

strips of fresh lime zest

1 Pour the milk and lime juice into a food processor and process gently until combined.

2 Add the kiwifruit and sugar and process gently, then add the ice cream and process until smooth. Pour the mixture into glasses and decorate with slices of fresh kiwifruit and strips of fresh lime zest. Serve at once.

Hazelnut & Coffee Sparkle

Try something a little different—you will be pleasantly surprised by the success of this delicious concoction.

INGREDIENTS

1 cup water

3 tbsp instant coffee crystals

½ cup sparkling water

1 tbsp hazelnut syrup

2 tbsp brown sugar

6 ice cubes

TO DECORATE

slices of fresh lime

slices of fresh lemon

1 Use the water and coffee crystals to brew some hot coffee, then let cool to room temperature (about 30 minutes). Transfer to a pitcher, cover with plastic wrap, and chill in the refrigerator for at least 45 minutes.

2 When the coffee has chilled, pour it into a food processor. Add the sparkling water, hazelnut syrup, and sugar, and process well. Add the ice cubes and process until smooth.

3 Pour the mixture into glasses, decorate the rims with slices of fresh lime and lemon, and serve.

Pineapple Soda

This is ice cream soda for grown-ups, a luscious mix of pineapple, coconut milk, and vanilla ice cream, which is irresistible.

SERVES 2

INGREDIENTS

¾ cup pineapple juice

scant ½ cup coconut milk

1 cup vanilla ice cream

1 cup frozen pineapple chunks

¾ cup sparkling water

2 scooped-out pineapple shells,
   to serve (optional)

1 Pour the pineapple juice and coconut milk into a food processor. Add the ice cream and process until smooth.

2 Add the pineapple chunks and process well. Pour the mixture into scooped-out pineapple shells or tall glasses, until two-thirds full. Top off with sparkling water, add straws, and serve.

Orange & Carrot Smoothie

This doesn't just taste and look fabulous, it also contains abundant health-giving beta-carotene and vitamin C.

INGREDIENTS

¾ cup carrot juice

¾ cup orange juice

¾ cup vanilla ice cream

6 ice cubes

TO DECORATE

slices of fresh orange

strips of fresh orange zest

1 Pour the carrot juice and orange juice into a food processor and process gently until well combined. Add the vanilla ice cream and process until thoroughly blended.

2 Add the ice cubes and process until smooth. Pour the mixture into glasses, decorate with slices of fresh orange and strips of fresh orange zest, and serve.

Pineapple & Coconut Shake

The perfect partnership—and a lovely way to wind down at the end of a busy day with your own perfect partner.

INGREDIENTS

1½ cups pineapple juice

scant ½ cup coconut milk

¾ cup vanilla ice cream

1 cup frozen pineapple chunks

2 scooped-out coconut shells,
   to serve (optional)

2 tbsp grated fresh coconut, to decorate

1 Pour the pineapple juice and coconut milk into a food processor. Add the ice cream and process until smooth.

2 Add the pineapple chunks and process until smooth. Pour the mixture into scooped-out coconut shells or tall glasses, and decorate with grated fresh coconut. Add straws and serve.

Caribbean Vegan Cocktail

Chill out with a tropical treat. If you close your eyes, you can almost hear the waves lapping on the beach.

SERVES 2

INGREDIENTS

scant ½ cup coconut milk

scant 1 cup soy milk

scant ½ cup pineapple juice

1 tbsp brown sugar

1 ripe mango, pitted and diced

2 tbsp grated fresh coconut

1 cup frozen pineapple chunks

1 banana, sliced and frozen

TO DECORATE

grated fresh coconut

wedges of fresh pineapple

1 Put the coconut milk, soy milk, pineapple juice, and sugar into a food processor and process gently until combined. Add the diced mango to the food processor along with the grated coconut and process well.

2 Add the frozen pineapple chunks and banana slices and process until smooth. Pour the mixture into glasses, scatter over some grated fresh coconut, and decorate the rims with wedges of fresh pineapple. Serve at once.

Red Storm

This sure-fire lip-smacker is a spicy little number and is definitely not for the unwary or faint-hearted.

SERVES 2

INGREDIENTS

2 cups tomato juice

dash of Worcestershire sauce

1 small red chile, seeded and chopped

1 scallion, trimmed and chopped

6 ice cubes

2 long, thin red chiles, cut into flowers
   (see step 1, below), to garnish

1 To make the chile flowers, use a sharp knife to make six cuts along each chile—place the point of the knife about ½ inch/1 cm from the stalk end and cut toward the tip. Put the chiles in a bowl of iced water and let them soak for 25–30 minutes, until they have spread out into flower shapes.

2 Put the tomato juice and Worcestershire sauce in a food processor and process gently until combined. Add the chopped chile, scallion, and ice cubes and process until smooth.

3 Pour the mixture into glasses and garnish with the chile flowers. Add straws and serve.

Hawaiian Shake

When your energy levels are flagging, give yourself
a treat with this invigorating and exuberant shake.

SERVES 2

I N G R E D I E N T S

1 cup milk

3½ tbsp coconut milk

¾ cup vanilla ice cream

2 bananas, sliced and frozen

1 cup canned pineapple chunks, drained

1 papaya, seeded and diced

T O   D E C O R A T E

grated fresh coconut

wedges of fresh pineapple

1 Pour the milk and coconut milk into a
food processor and process gently
until combined. Add half of the vanilla ice
cream and process gently, then add the
remaining vanilla ice cream and process
until smooth.

2 Add the frozen banana slices and
process well, then add the pineapple
chunks and papaya and process until
smooth. Pour the mixture into tall glasses,
scatter over the grated coconut, and
decorate the rims with pineapple wedges.
Serve at once.

Rose Sunset

This beautifully fragrant drink, with its romantic name, has an equally delectable and illusive flavor.

SERVES 2

INGREDIENTS

scant ½ cup plain yogurt

2 cups milk

1 tbsp rose water

3 tbsp honey

1 ripe mango, pitted and diced

6 ice cubes

edible rose petals, to decorate (optional)

1 Pour the yogurt and milk into a food processor and process gently until combined.

2 Add the rose water and honey and process until thoroughly blended, then add the mango along with the ice cubes and process until smooth. Pour the mixture into glasses, decorate with edible rose petals, if using, and serve.